STEPHEN ROMER was born in Hertfordshire in 1957 and educated at Trinity Hall, Cambridge. Since 1981 he has lived in France, where he is Maître de Conférences in the English department of Tours University. He has been three times Visiting Professor in French at Colgate University, New York. Stephen Romer has published three previous collections of poetry with Oxford University Press and is the editor of the Faber anthology *Twentieth-Century French Poems*. A selection of his recent poems appeared in the Carcanet Oxford*Poets* anthology 2001, and a book of his selected poems in French translation, *Tribut*, was published by Éditions le temps qu'il fait in 2007. He regularly writes on French literature and modern poetry for the *Guardian* and the *Times Literary Supplement*.

Also by Stephen Romer

*Idols*
*Plato's Ladder*
*Tribute*

As editor
*Twentieth-Century French Poems*

STEPHEN ROMER

# *Yellow Studio*

Oxford*Poets*

**CARCANET**

First published in Great Britain in 2008 by
Carcanet Press Limited
Alliance House
Cross Street
Manchester M2 7AQ

A CIP catalogue record for this book is available from the British Library
ISBN 978 1 903039 85 4

The publisher acknowledges financial assistance from Arts Council England

Typeset by XL Publishing Services, Tiverton
Printed and bound in England by SRP Ltd, Exeter

*for my Mother*

# Acknowledgements

Grateful acknowledgement is made to the editors of the following magazines and journals in which many of these poems first appeared: *European English Messenger* (ESSE), the *Financial Times*, the *London Magazine*, *Modern Poetry in Translation*, *New Writing 10*, *PN Review*, *Poetry Review*, *The Spectator*, *Stand* and the *Times Literary Supplement*.

'Stand-To' first appeared in *After the Storm*, a pamphlet edited by Peter Balakian and Hank Lewis (Colgate University, NY 2005).

A further group of poems was published in *Ezra Pound: Language and Persona*, edited by Massimo Bacigalupo and William Pratt (proceedings of the XXI Convegno Internazionale di Studi su Ezra Pound, held in Rapallo in July 2005).

My translations of Apollinaire are from his collections *Calligrammes*, *Il y a* and *Poèmes à Lou*.

# Contents

## 1

## 2

# 3

# 4

# 5   An Enthusiast

*1*

## Recognition

You were right, righter than you thought, when you asked,
curious at my excess, and *ingénue*,
'Do I remind you of someone?'

Well, yes and no... Something ancient
and new at once, old anima stirring
in her cave, the power of the Name,

calling back through the fields of corn
to Naomi and her daughters, to something
sacred, and I could not answer, instead

there were tears, along with tequilas,
when tilted by a giant hand
I leaned to plant the longest kiss,

as the two phlegmatic zitherers
sat like dummies side by side
and plucked out Zorba's table-dancing kitsch...

After the colour-coding and the blusher
after the Matisse tattoo
after the touch of sprinkle-glitter

(gilding the lily that, if ever)
– there were tears, tears, the true ones, of joy,
(bottle them, bottle them, for later).

# At the Procope

Yes, the giant prawns have eyes! Black
threaded nodules, to stare you through...
Take it away, take it away, their little bodies!

was how she greeted our not inexpensive
seafood platter, though she fairly speared
the whelks and chewed an oyster or two

and made a face, gulping down a *calva*
like medicine – my dear, I see the gaps
in your West and East coast grooming...

(*How insufferable he is – he wants to kiss*
*the honeyed ramparts at my ear*
*– even that comes out of Yeats!*

*And patronising with it, he drivels*
*like a dotard, worse, the proverbial*
*anecdotard, a word in the OED, he said,*

*and all that silly Muse stuff, the angel,*
*the anima, the shock of recognition,*
*Flaubert's 'ce fut comme une apparition' –*

*just to hook up with me –*
*I told him it was burdensome,*
*and I don't even swing that way!*)

– though to be kind, she's only just turned legal
in that peculiar throwback of a country,
at least as far as drinking is concerned,

and then she does something amazing,
she rises in the restaurant, and lowers
her jeans in front of the gawping diners

to show me a snatch of Stevens – was it
*The Idea of Order?* – indelibly tattooed
on her back, just along the pantyline.


## Alas Without Constraint


Having a Coke with you
          in the *Coffee Parisien*
has got to be more fun
          than trailing to an exhibition
even Picasso's *érotique*;
          and pausing with you by the café
where Perec wrote
          *tentative d'épuisment d'un lieu parisien*
is more thrilling
          than *littérature à contraintes*;
I'd rather you took me shopping
          for a pair of two-tone shoes,
and I've never been less in the mood
          and more in need
of decorum
          and a bit of restraint
and of saying less
          and meaning more,
and of everything I preached
          but cannot practise
let alone stretched out with you
          flat on the bookshop floor
with Berryman's *Sonnets*
          'volleying blue air'
because indestructible lightheartedness
          is upon me
whose sweet rare source
          was blindingly there

# Swallow

*Strana sorella*, you came and went
in one parabola,
a swallow dipping

through my window
and out with all
your promise intact.

Sunflowers at the pupil,
curls of the willow,
a raspberry capping a finger,

green-violet
tints-in-silk, a swarthy face
with dimples I could have lived in.

You were two weekends
of that joy again!
And as suddenly

recalled,
by one more serious than I.
'Sincere', was your word. *Addio.*

## Yehuda Halevi to His Love: A Remonstration

'Lovely doe, you pause to wonder
if my devotion is constructed
or available to others –

to your talkative friend, for instance,
who sat between us
"oozing charm and poise"?

Even were it so,
when you disappear
for weeks without a word

hidden in your veil and jellabah
– the Jewish maid decked out an Arab –
I ask you this:

Where do you suppose
my devotion can go?
Must I also change religion

to meet you in the Mosque
(strange trysting-place indeed
to test our sacred Recognition!)

As you learn the faith
of others, have a little faith,
I pray you, in my own.'

# Senex

*'…he could not get rid of the tendency to reconstruct the "Ange"*
*who was daily broken into fragments…'*

Italo Svevo, *Senility*

As I wrap your photograph
with its expensive frame
back into the crêpe
and then the paper

deciding I cannot
go through this again
the stupid vertigo
at the merest sign of life

the stain in the mind's eye
that tarnishes the rest
the dreary ache
of the unrequited

– hoping to nip
that nonsense in the bud
I find nevertheless
my lips pressed to the paper

in the region I suppose of your heart
thus re-inventing
an orthodox gesture,
the kissing of the Icon

that I wrap and hide and thereby find
to be my satisfaction,
the worship
not even you can forbid.

## Cut-off Point

Once it was the angel above Teresa
stabbing her into ecstasy

now it is the look of loving regret
as of someone who has tried hard

but must at last bring down the sword
as Caravaggio's David

brought down the sword
wistfully lopping the head

of his shaggy incorrigible
slavering devotee.

## Recidivist

So this is how it ends:
at a corner table
in a stale café
on the boulevard of abulia.
With a small jug of tepid water
and the eternal Lipton's teabag
laid genteelly on the saucer.

To slake our ten-year thirst.

You will not stay.
And I as always
have a train for the provinces.

Even the turn of your calf
is enough to make me ache.
The way your blue dress rises.

# St Stephen

*for Hugo Williams*

*'We couldn't talk about love the other night,*
*but I assume you are doomed, also?'*


I got your card: Stephen bowed
asking for the *coup de grâce* –
a point-blank boulder coming from behind.

And come it does: she's wed.

For ten years in the wings
she bore my comings and goings
my disappearance in the crowd.

Gently, gently, she lets me down.

Now I'm cast in Gothic
I hope I can be gracious,
dignified, courteous, kind.

I hope I can carry my head
with a rock
encrusting it like a crown.

## Even Now

I dreamed I was driving to see you
alone in your moated house

but I noted on approach I was steering
from the back seat, apparently,

with no one at the wheel...
I thought it might be possible

even now to coast up to your door
without a mortal accident.

So no change there, you'll say.
The uncontrollable want

grafted on
to reckless temporisation.

# Love and the Name

*'Like rays from a nucleus, the existence of the loved one proceeds from her name,
and even the works created by the lover proceed from the same source.'*

Walter Benjamin

When I speak the names
they compose a mantra
I have sobbed or murmured
in the night.

The lullaby of their names
neither shortened nor sweetened
is suddenly solemn
like the Aleph or the Om:

the fount of clear water
the saint of music
the golden stone

– names you wear so lightly,
my lost ones, when each
rhymes ecstasy with pain.

# Ascension Day

One entire Ascension Day
glued to the earth
hunched against a radiator

reading *La fugitive*
like a fugue, where death
is the theme, *elle ne revint jamais*

as if time could be halted
in the heart of a paragraph, with the entire
giving over of the self

to mourning and desire,
to stasis, to the abolition
of time, her time and mine,

as long as I went on reading, re-reading,
no harm could come
to anyone, nothing could be transformed

and nothing could move on,
or be forgotten,
destroyed, or built upon.

# Figment

## 1

I bow to Him, and bow to Him;
for bowing breaks the thought stream.

The wind in trees. That is a beginning
and an end. Refuge on refuge.

Stopped at source. Not desire
but the knowledge of desiring.

I send the sutras to all and sundry and preach
what I cannot practise.

## 2

The temptation of symbolic orders
came to me again:

a peacock imago on Shelley's page.
As I read with jaundiced eye

how he meets, in human guise,
the moonlike idol of his thought,

there was this irreducible creature,
woken from the dark, and sunning

beneath the scholar's lamp, Epipsychidion,
his love, his wraith, his mind.

# Sidney Sussex Chapel

*for Claire and Kevin Jackson*

Faces moulded in the candlelight,
loved and loving faces, all of them
friends, and all intent, in this minute
of sweet and solemn introit,
happiness running like a current –

And now our clever friends
are this man and this woman

necks bowed
      on the altar step –
hands joined, wrapped in a stole

and held aloft

by another friend who cries
*Let no man put asunder*


We are exalted,
          and cast down,
by that burning shower of coal the Prayer Book.

No mistaking, we stand rebuked.

*2*

# Dismantling the Library

The removal of the honeycomb
or the hornet's nest
layer by layer

is not what I thought, I did not say
this is my store, my sweetness,
my distillate, I did not feel
that here, at least,
I am lord of all I survey

but noted rather, dismayingly,
how many had lain unread
like this *Modern Turkish Poetry*
or this un-put-down-able Life of Tolstoy,

and how even the lovely foxed familiars
retired behind their covers
as if I had to begin again
and come upon them as a stranger.

# Dismantlings 2

The little room dismantled, returned
to cobwebs that, to be frank, haven't moved
in fourteen years, gothic drapes by now.
A sign of my passage –
the carpet worn threadbare
beneath the desk;
22 cartons of papers
and 500 books
unstrung from its gut.
Scarcely rentable like this,
but squattable tomorrow
by strangers.
Some blanker passages
on the wall, a few nails,
the crude plaster that still draws blood
if you graze against it,
the parchment walls
I have layered with nicotine,
all that remains
of the blue pall
that moved beyond the margins
of the green-shaded lamp
who comes, however, along with me.

# A Thought from Petronius

*for Robert Wells*

At the end of the day
even urbane Petronius
Imperial Arbiter of Taste
craved no more than this:

a cot, a loaded applebough,
a vat of the local plonk,
a pair of elms to sling a hammock,
and a massive gate and lock

to keep the *res publica* at bay.


# A Small Field

A small field to autumn cyclamen
given up in slantlight, a thicket
of individual lights, the groomed balsam,
the barbed acacia drops her leaves
in a squall, strong weak light, October light,
the precious dregs, the late squibs,
the rapid dripping from the gutter.

A landfall of cloud, brushed up,
blue-violet breasting the Loire,
and the harvest brought down
from the hill, the camber running
reddish and ferment in the vats,
a sour tang, immutable summer
crushed underfoot now, as in *cru*.

# Loire, August

Solitude here is not the driven wandering
through a city, but goes deep,
is actually sweet, and is wide as walls
over one yard thick: here a man
can feel the solid chalk beneath his feet,
and wake to the sound of woodpigeons calling
and a light summer rain on the sycamores.
Somewhere down there is the river,
where the terns skim and tumble
threading braids of sand, and fishermen
unchanged since the start of *congés payés*
drop a languid hook, and their womenfolk chat on
in the shade of willows or a white van,
and assorted children fill with their noise
a sunny abeyance: *Les grandes vacances.*

## 'Bonne femme d'intérieur'

In this heart of the heart
of the country
there's little by way of temptation...

I checked the personals, and found,
along with a boiler given away,
and firewood, as much as you can carry,

a host of women, a phalanx
of the over-sixty-fives, enduring widows
of vintners, weathered as *vieux ceps*,

offering what they have, the basics,
to keep a man warm at night,
and by day, to give him shade.

# Days of Oestrus

She stalked me
for a year, for a year
I held out, and behold:

a potlatch of toms
sit round her in a ring
with ears pricked

as she rolls among the snowdrops
to rub off his smell
and shows her belly

to urge another on.
She licks the place
and squirms and rolls

what a performance
polite and attentive
the toms wait their turn.

They fled from me
who regard me now
as they might a shadow

a no-man a nothing
no match for them
no match for her, and how

they come around
they come around
the days of oestrus!

And the toms have fucked off
and she mewls at my door
about our future.

# Fantasy Life

Surely potting petunias
is as innocent an occupation

as any, even in man's first garden.
Absorbed with mulch and trowel

for an hour or so, I forgot you.
But glancing now, through the open door,

at my full-bottomed urn in the twilight
parti-shadowed by the watering

the flesh-coloured clay has divided
for all the world

into Mlle O'Murphy's buttocks

complete with handles.

# Canto Lalagen

*for Jamie McKendrick*

*Salve*, Lalage

I raise a glass
of the *Roses du Clos*
to where she gathers
her gown at the lawn's end

staring at the god
priapic among birches
she is serene
where now the Diluvian laves her

or else under chafing Dog Star
*atrox hora Caniculae*
or in the bitter Ligerian,
or the riverine damp, she stands

*hic in reducta valle*
where I left a shears
in the creeper, at the zenith
of a teetering ladder

and only Faunus saved me
from falling to my death
her graces also
interceding

whom now Apollo favours
with slantlight on her belly
and gives since her arrival
a new dispensation

of light and space
guiding and dividing
till all rays lead to her
my *ridens* if not *loquens*

Lalage, *salve!*

# Forty-Something

*Anno domini*, behave accordingly,
with dignity, and pruned expectation.

Your Bible is
Dr D.G. Hessayon's *Bedding Plant Expert*
and your lusts are
Albertine,
Ghislaine de Féligonde
and Mme Alfred Carrière.

How well they look,

manured and settled,
if a little blowsy after rain.

# The Repartee

Clinched in a *slow,* the aging Don
with an *égérie* not yet twenty
is thinking of self-reform, i.e.
this is the last, this is the one,

and whispers to himself, or to her
(that much remains uncertain)
come away, O come away,
the two of us together, *hein?*

Come to where an occasional
breeze fingers at the curtain
our limbs arranged in a still
heavier sweetness, this is the deep

siesta of my life, I'm listening
to my new, my newly faithful heart!
*'Monsieur?... Monsieur!*
*Il est tard. Il faut que je parte.'*

# Metamorphosis

*Albert Mérat, one of the* Vilains Bonshommes, *the circle to which Verlaine and, briefly, Rimbaud belonged, requested that Fantin-Latour paint him out of the group portrait* Un Coin de Table, *fearing his reputation would be tarnished.*

Poor Albert Mérat,
*le grand Albert,*
the elegant, the choleric,
the neurasthenic,
known to his friends as
'the scornful cigar'
met his nemesis
in a baby-faced terror
stalking in from the countryside
with huge hands and huge feet
burning up the foothills
of Young Parnassus.
Genius came at poor Albert
with a sneer and a sword-stick.

He too had his sensitive *Chimères*
praised by *l'oncle Hugo,*
he too had his ode to the anus
censured by Lemerre –
he too his promising beginnings.
He too wore his pen down
and then walked out
of a dreary sinecure.
Wit, wag, *Zutiste à ses heures,*
ladies man, gossip, poet, poseur.
Yet of Albert Mérat
who took fright
nothing is left
but a pot of flowers.

# A Bridgehead of Sorts

'But passion is indulgent, selfish,
compared say to –

anyway, what do you mean by unconditional love?'
asks my son, a tyro in philosophy,

guiding the discussion with a firm hand
away from fuzziness, dispersion, quotation,

– vices of the unmethodical mind.
He requires a definition

and all we can give him are instances…
He is, on the whole, unmoved by these

till someone ventures 'it's to do with procreation' –
which seems a breakthrough

though we can't persuade him (we the old lags)
that passion can make us love the world

and the world us
(that quick shy smile again, deferent-sardonic?)

– showing himself thus unacquainted
with the subject of his scepticism,

but pleased with what we do establish: a start,
a bridgehead of sorts.

# Young Man

Young man, with a table and a shelf
and Gray's *Anatomy*, setting out
to grasp the trunk of knowledge

and lead the examined life,
perched above the Unjust City
in his nine square metres,

rapt in Spinoza,
or moving like an open knife
among the haltered populace

in thrall to its own implacable:
we receive his discourse
as we would the muzzle

of the antlered deer who wanders down
to pluck at the ancient apple-tree
and is so quick to fear.

## Stand-To

*'Jardin où saigne abondamment le laurier rose fleur guerrière…'*
Apollinaire

This garden everywhere
is transfigured for minutes on end
after rain, a breach in the west,
russet light solid on the trees and walls

and on the squat church tower.
How many did the village lose?
Evening after evening, bearing arms
against a livid afterglow,

he missed the church bell, and the harvest
in the vineyard overhead
the year of the heat-wave
that killed the old, the year of the *grand cru.*

He comes home, at this moment, pauses
in this precise light, and then
descends the old stone steps,
slowly as from a podium.

# Four from Apollinaire

## Platoon Leader

My mouth will have the fires of Gehenna
My mouth will be a hell of sweetness and seduction
The angels of my mouth will lord it in your heart
The soldiers of my mouth will rout you
The priests of my mouth will cense your beauty
Your soul will tremble like salients in an earthquake
And then your eyes will brim
                With all the love there has ever been
In human eyes from the beginning
My mouth will raise an army against you
An army of irregulars
Various like an enchanter who knows how to shift his shapes
The choirs and orchestras of my mouth will declare my love
(It murmurs to you from far away)
As I stand with my eyes fixed upon my watch
                Waiting for the moment we go over.

## Cornflower

Young man
Twenty years old
You have seen such horrors
What do you think
Of your childhood mentors now

You know
The bravura and the guile

You
Have
Seen
Death
Up
Close
More
Than
One
Hundred
Times
You
Do
Not
Know
What
Life
Is

Pass your braveness on
To those who come
After

Young man
You are joyful your memory is bloodied
Red too your soul
With joy
You have absorbed the life of those who died around you
You are decisive
It is seventeen hundred hours and you will know

How to die
If not better than your elders
More piously without a doubt
Since you know of death more than life
O sweetness of a different age
Agelessly drawn out

# Epithalamium in Orange

*for Anne and Christopher Page*

Do you recall the basket of oranges
Sweet as the love we made at the time
You sent them on a wintry day to Nîmes
Gold fruit of angels I dared not eat them

I kept them for ages so we'd eat them together
When you came to Nîmes when you came to Nîmes
In vain I waited in the tatters of my love
And the oranges softened my Heart I waited

One little orange remained intact
I took it with me up the Line
And here it is still safe and sound
Compacted round and small

Among the falling shells I eat it
Delicious as my Love from Nîmes
O concentrated Sun rich as my Rhyme
O sweet-tasting Love my little orange

Such memories are juice on the lips
Eating it I forgot my tatters
And thought of my Love my Love in Nîmes
And ate it all up flesh rind and pips

Think of that orange from time to time
Sweet as the love as the love from Nîmes
Now that you've come my Love to Nîmes
Think of that orange
                    From time to time

# Hill 146

No flowers left but strange signs
gesturing down the blue nights
in my prolonged adoration Lou
my whole being bows down
with the low clouds of July
before your memory

It is a white plaster head
buried helplessly next a golden ring
and our promises are remoter echoes
they sound sometimes strangely

Listen there is a permanent white noise
my caustic solitude is lit up only
by the far powerful searchlight my love
I can hear the bass voice of Big Bertha

And down by the trenches
in front of me a cemetery
has been sown
with forty-six-thousand soldiers
after such sowings we must
wait with serenity for harvest

                    If ever there were desolation
it is here where I write my letter
leaning on a slab of asbestos
I keep looking at your portrait
the one with the wide hat

Some of my comrades have seen your photo
and assuming that I know you
they ask who is she
and I can't quite think what to say
seeing as even now I hardly know you

Which pierces me
and deep inside the photograph
you are smiling still like light

*3*

# Retour au pays

## 1

Waking to the radio. Its level voices
tell me something has altered, that this
is my other country, and it is like
a comfort less, something in the rhythm
and the pitch that sets my teeth on edge,
something harder and more pragmatic
like a floor uncarpeted, or is it
a throwback to that wall-eyed bedsit
where I woke to voices like these, to nerves,
and to the wreckers with hammer and drill
dismantling the building about my head.
Whatever it is, the sound has distilled
my dislike. Something brisk, and matter-of-fact,
abrasive and technically perfect.

Now I'm driving through the mind
of a polytechnician, on a level plain
criss-crossed with runways and arterials
fraught with traffic, a glinting array
of juggernauts, the gnomic *Olloquiegi*
blazoned on their sides. They are silent,
and a white impassive armorial sun
elongates our shadows. The fluidity
of flyover and underpass and interchange,
the thrill of this untrammeled movement
into and around the intelligent heart
of Europe! The abstract towers wink
and beckon across the ice. I'll take the risk.
*Amour! Qu'avons-nous fait de nous mêmes!*

*'J'ai longtemps habité Montmartre; on y jouit d'un air très pur...'*

Nerval

Returning here
under the cold blue
the rue des Saules
is absurdly tender
with its pink house
on the corner
and the Château des Brouillards
with its ruined vineyard
and its secret trees
still a world on its own
while in the little bookshop
on the rue Ravignan
are back issues of reviews
we read when we were young
and every *bouquiniste*
gave up treasures
the one leading to the next
as the deep streets of the Butte
led towards a light
as if cast upward by the sea

# Bras de fer

*Aux armes, citoyens!*
Man the barricades!
Your sea-green Jacobin
has risen again

to counter the vulpine
spectre of modernity
with his whitewolf hair
and his toothy smile.

This is the mystic Hexagon
where nothing starts
and nothing ends
in the basilisk stare

of State and Citizen.
Left, Right, Left, Right
we march without moving
and it's always '89.

# École des Hautes Études

The Professor of Political Science
and his colleagues
handed the key to the People,

with a slap at Police 'brutality'...
Now he gapes, almost touchingly
bewildered

to find his Temple of Reason
besmirched by the People
and on his desk

an incontrovertible turd.
'But how can one instruct
such mindlessness,

this is merely Barbarism!'
He is startled to find
rising in his nostrils

a smell he will disown
as the stench could it be
of Clerical Treason.

But he says his piece,
he always does, articulate soul,
'This is Police Conspiracy!'

# The Professor of Ideas

*'Nature is sublimed'*
Student exam paper

'Wordsworth in the Alps,
Frankenstein on the *mer de glace*,
Shelley scribbling his graffiti
*atheos, demokratikos, philanthropos,*
somewhere below Mont Blanc,

that massive abstract breast –
all this talk! They stretch and yawn
and challenge with turquoise eyes,
a row of plunging *décolletées*,
the seven Ravines of the Arve!

I speak more and more of "gender",
of penetrative science
and incestuous necrophilia,
of the repressed and weeping
silent Eve,

of climactic evolution,
the vigorous coupling of mammals
as crucial to health,
I recall the Eternal Feminine
– by now I'm nearly pleading.

I summon the female monster
from the workshop of dirty creation,
*Frankenstein's Daughter*
rising with gigantic organs
to beget upon men,

I'm thumping the desk,
an evangelical homunculus
among the fleshpots,
a monster, an angel with horns,
issuing smoke and imprecation

as they file out cool as you please
leaving their ravages behind,
the male hypercephalus
consumed in a self-made fire
dying out at last among his books.'

# The Conjuror

In an airtight room
the conjuror in glasses
draws his nets
round the thrashing fish of the poem.

Its bones and flesh and scales
are signs and drives and tropes
are semes and themes and isotopes.
The sun makes angles on the walls

this mid-afternoon in Lyon
where nature corrects her curvature
and the Rhône and the Saône flow straight
like axes in a theorem.

The conjuror in glasses
chopping and fitting
squeezes the fish through a grid.
And then it vanishes.

# Farewell to an Idea

*on reading T.J. Clark*

Arrive one morning in the south
train-worn into the mimosa
and walk through our joyful misprision,
the sensual life of art
stirring the grids of winter.

How details are edible!
The hill above Céret
is a sliced watermelon
and we sit bemused, in sunlight,
under a giant plane tree

where the local painter is holding forth,
and Picasso has left his mark
like a rogue tomcat,
his musky signature
displayed by the *patron*.

The café Mazagran, the Marc,
the tonic Armagnac, the Pernod,
the crystal carafe in reversible cubes,
vestigial sleeves, complicit buttons,
dredged up in those nets

or cast ashore from the shipwreck
glinting and winking;
and young we sat down on a bench
to talk it through, we were in love
with the dissolution

barely held at bay, those recognitions
our comfort and our constraint.
*Mere ghostly differentials*, says
the Critic, and we are old, and exiled
into more frightening country.

# Ermenonville

So it once was, so it is again,
for a single afternoon,

on our bikes, wheels silted up with sand
in the desert of Ermenonville

where the fire girls float their wraiths
at the vague ends of avenues.

They were goblins of melancholy
there among the ferns,

they were sirens, and drove me mad.
This time, for sanity, I pocketed

a pine kernel, to have and to hold,
while you rode ahead

on the path to Mortefontaine
where Corot painted in silver-fleck,

past the well in the road
with its clear-standing water.

This time the eyes were yours
and only yours, sweet tilted,

meeting mine across the years
and your hair *en chignon*, and you straight-backed

and beautiful of carriage
as when I glimpsed you way back when,

papoose strapped in behind you,
cycling decidedly out of my life.

# Jardin Anglais: A Malentendu for Two Voices

*'Les galeries du cloître, la chapelle aux ogives élancées, la tour féodale et le petit château qui abrita les amours de Henri IV et de Gabrielle se teignaient des rougeurs du soir sur le vert sombre de la forêt.'*

*'Vous êtes une nymphe antique qui vous ignorez...'*

Gérard de Nerval, *Sylvie*

*Et Chenonceau, Mesdames, c'est surtout
le château de l'amour adultère!*

Inside the house, I preserve my space,
I dart into doorways and linger in stairwells.
When they walk overhead in the airy chambers
I'm below stairs among the roasting spits.
I left him showing a dubious Correggio,
and three nubile graces with boudoir eyes.
At least it keeps his mind off me.
I pass through a gallery of swords and pikes.
The glass is weeping in the window
where I stand in an alcove, looking out
or looking in. Is it me, or is it the world
walled up in glass? If only I could touch it!
Now this I like, Catherine's little reading room
athwart the river, queen of her domain,
centre of the hive, with a massive door and lock,
but here's our 'guide', breathing down my neck
to murmur something half-historical.

*Ah, Mademoiselle, vous voilà
I thought you'd gone and died of love!
Do you see, over the mantelpiece,
the tierce intertwined, and set in tufa?
That rogue! With his ménage à trois
established forever in graffiti,
Diane – Henri – Catherine.
I wonder... I forget...
was his blazon goat or porcupine?
And have you seen the creepy bedroom?*

Creepy, he says. I find it moving,
this mourning room done out in pale greys,
with a motif of thorns and a vessel
to receive silver tears. Perhaps the death's head
a little overdone. There's a doll-sized bed
where the grieving queen laid out her corpse
and arranged her hands. Civilisation must allow
a place for the heartbroken and the hurt by life!
'The widowed queen would spend her days
in prayer and fasting.' I sympathise.

*Mademoiselle, I'm sorry to intrude,*
*but now we go to see the gardens, maybe*
*not your style, too French and mise en ordre,*
*nature brutally arraigned, too much*
*geometry! But you'll like the trees, flowing free,*
*and the roses are spectacular, we have*
*the latest climber, Ghislaine de Féligonde,*
*perhaps another royal mistress?*

He's right, I like the moors, and weather,
not the formal hothouse of Le Nôtre.
These trees are fine, avenues elegant,
his conversation mildly interesting
when he lays his own *galanterie* aside.
But on our way to see the roses
– oh god, no peace –
'*Les Dames sont embusquées par Silénus,*
*Mademoiselle, beware the satyrs!*'
and sure enough a rout of leering fauns
is peeping round the urns, on the path
to the spouting grotto…

*...a good example of Italianate*
*mechanics... and that's Apollo, fed and watered*
*by three compliant daughters,*
*the local aristocracy, you see,*
*taking turns*
*to amuse a bloated monarch.*
*You see he is incorr-i-gi-ble!*
*Maybe for that, we should chop his head,*
*eh Mademoiselle?*

I would plead for the stifled queen
craving light. Visited
with childbirth after childbirth.
To hell with his heartless
artifice. She commanded mirrors
reflecting windows, mirrors
not eyes. Endlessly caressed by eyes,
here on my plinth. Why will they
look at me not listen to me?
How they resent what they prize
in themselves, lucidity, control.
The nymph has lowered her eyes,
her urn pours copious water.
Here is Niobe, weeping
herself into the fountain,
Canens, crying herself
into the stream. Here is Echo
with her tongue cut out.

*4*

# Getting Educated at MOMA

*for Masha*

*Et nous sommes dans une autre sphère*
*Une autre salle*
*Sous un autre climat*

Pierre Reverdy


You educate my gaze
in front of Matisse's
little rose table
that tilts unpromisingly and has
an unappealing object some kind of bag
angled awkwardly
on its surface
this is discomfiting
and salutary

while the surface
of Monet's water-lilies
is easy, viscous,
no structure no backbone
and the slime it disguises
oozes up from underneath
the seats we're sitting on
for this, apparently,
is the Bourgeois Room.

Either side, Bonnard's windows
with their framing devices
and loving views
give on to the good life
– all I ever wanted
or thought art was –
now disabused
by your grainy childhood
in a satellite of Leningrad.

But later, in your grey
and lemon outfit,
you describe to me
with a certain satisfaction
over the arugula
how one of your exes
compared you
tiresomely
to the nudes of Modigliani.

# Yellow Studio

Vuillard's studio, Château des Clayes…
The corner is hard to judge
where the paintings in the painting are pinned
on the yellow wall (the *mise en abyme*
will be the end of me)

in this gleaming Institute of Donors,
this imperial temple
raised from the muck and blood
of the stockyards, out of hog-squeal
and cost-efficient slaughter

at the end of Millennium Park
where the towers crowd and crane
in an ogre's silver egg,
the concentration of capital
in a cunning device.

I stare with nostalgia, with homesickness
into Vuillard's yellow studio
and I know the place
absolutely, it is that humane
heaven of drapes and turpentine

where I shall at last lie down
on the lumpy mattress
with the stripy bedspread
below the little skylight –
my sweet, autarchic rest.

# A Transcendental Weekend

It seemed the best was a weekend ban
on images and news, when every time
a plane came over we saw the towers
gashed and smoking... A ban on CNN.

A return to Nature capital N,
with the Reverend Ripley, he of Brook Farm,
or Emerson's eyeball on Concord common
one snowy evening, *glad to the brink of fear*,

and the great man scourging and urging
the thrifty farm-folk hereabouts
to look around them and discover
that love of beauty is not effeminate...

We were pioneers – for a brief span –
the time it took to paddle across a lake
in a sweet warm wind of early autumn
and set foot upon the virgin sand

of a fly-infested inlet – our pantisocracy!
We were polyandrous, an Eve
with two Adams, actually a scandal
to the godfearing bearhunters

who baffled and kindly say grace
before meals in the candlelight and fly
Old Glory from every porch and post
– communal living an iniquity,

Babylon at the foot of Mount Hurricane.
... Or let us be shipwrecked, and cast up
further back, before the Founding Fathers,
on an island of magic that hurts not.

# Today I must teach Voltaire

Today I must teach Voltaire
to sorrowing sophomores,
I must teach the Enlightenment
in a toxic darkness

where yesterday the *Infâme*
flew sweet and level by Ellis Island
into Paradise. And the priests and analysts
who frightened themselves in the nursery

with ghouls and goblins,
till Spiderman in leotards swung down
to tuck them in, are everywhere on hand
to counsel the grieving sophomores;

and here is a President
sitting among children in a classroom,
with his reading book upside down.
He must explain to all of the children

this blazing love of death.

# Adirondacks

What price *ostranenie*? Strangers we are
on this road, in this hamlet, ghost hamlet,
that seems somehow to begin, then peter out,
after the diner,
the taxidermist,
the storefront stuffed with furry animals,
the weirdly talkative optometrist...

Settled in 18-something, barely settled, more perched,
a rocker on a ramshackle porch
on a capsized clapboard –
the place has seen the pilgrims off
with its drained look –
livid or pallid or aghast, whatever
that look *is* after months of being smothered,

with its tints of grey and yellow,
dying or reviving, death-in-life or
life-in-death... Near to, the roadside trees
have an ashen look,
and lean upon each other like survivors
who have come a long way
and want a lift... These are the violet groves

unfolding this Interior
where we push on through, and stop, in the shocked air,
by a lake so unloved it has a number
not a name, and returns our fear,
as though something happened here,
massacre or casual roadkill,
our jolly picnic withers on the stem.

But there's room at the Inn,
plenty of room and a smiley welcome,
'Things are a bit slow, folks stay home,
we call this really the in-between,
in-between the skiing and the boating...'
She brings us pancakes, and tea
in a urine bottle. Another misunderstanding.

We inspect the Victorian parlour
with its furnishings and chintz,
fussy, waxed, unhappy,
cozy as the Sabbath.
In the musty lobby
a moose's head and a black bear
discuss the One that Got Away.

Above the bar, a toupéed evangelist
exhorts his captive audience
of the palsied and the lame –
'You must have Feet of Iron, see,
not Feet of Clay, nor even Feet
of Clay and Iron mixed, but Feet of Iron
to get to Heaven!'

So we walk the straitened track,
masses of unbroken ice
creaking on either side – that fear again –
when out of nowhere, phantom church bells,
sweet, off-key, unplaceable,
sprinkle balm
on the body of Leviathan.

# Poets in the Academy

Deep summer in the woods,
or the swamp;

the poets stumble out
with their incomprehensible produce.

Now they must lay it down
for comparison and analysis

as the maples start to burn
and the freshman snivels.

They must don white coats
and turn to the taxonomist

– Professor Jakobson!
Pray let us blow the dust off of you,

come stand outside the forest
with a map and compass

please to remind us
and our sullen disciples

what modes of address
we have employed

what salient features
we have moved among.

# Waindell Shorts

## 1

Candy the Flake
from Brooklyn
drives a Chevy SUV
(*we call her Big Red*)
and screamed at Marcel Duchamp
dressed as Rose Sélavy
*THAT's not a woman!*
Candy found DADA
inadequate as art
but the furry saucepan
I brought into class, now that –
that was *AWESOME!*

## 2

Hearing Holly, brunette,
and Lux, blonde

exploring in duet
*Un amour de Swann*

the synaesthesias of *the little phrase*
Odette's nestling cattleyas

I was lost for a minute
in the fragrant contiguities

*But he doesn't love her,*
*he doesn't even know her –*
*he just, like, wants a girlfriend*
they opine.

## 3

Faced with Dali's
anamorphic Masturbator,
the meats, the tufts, the clefts,
Darlene exclaims
*My God that's a belly-button!*

At which, laidback Laura from Quebec:

*Belly-button my arse,*
*for Chrissake get me outta here!*


## 4
## For Your Own Safety

*Nina*

Even as three fat officers
with chains and walkie-talkies
squawking out their arses
piled in from Campus Safety

followed by the fire officer
and a brace of electricians
to undo the shambles
of their state-of-the-art warning system

the imperturbable Professor of Russian
who set off the smoke alarm
and then the fire alarm
stirred her ferocious curry.

# Senior Year Portrait

*'Now I guess I must stop and get on with my work. I wrote nothing but poetry for*
*two days after I came back, but none of it is fit to be seen yet.'*

Elizabeth Bishop at Vassar

A girl in a bolt of silk
climbs down a fire-escape
and walks barefoot in the wet:
the maples blow about her
the deep reds blow about her
as she moves among the sprinklers
and lays her body down
on the campus lawn:
*My need to be alone.*

The lasting goldenrod
chicory and aster
the swoop and flop of a Monarch
the crimson in the cambers
load every rift
as she would load her life
*I shall live there*
*deeply, every instant*
*of every day.*
The focus hard

the future Fulbright.
*Joy and poetry and connecting*
*are my three things in life*
even on this memorial day
– O College America –
careers go on,
the photo in the Yearbook,
*Is that me? O-my-God!*
Next year's abroad.
And then: New York.

11 September 2002

## Shibbutz and Iqtibas

*for Gabriel Levin*

I was to join you, Gabriel, on one of your
sundazed forays to Judea – eyes half-closed in the heat,
slouch hat back from your forehead,
your lithe indolence, allusive brilliance
re-inhabiting the Empty Quarter
with humanist poets, composers of *Qasida*,
lovesick but alive
to the teeming minuscule life of the desert.
I would have gone with you to Jericho,
you and your gathering-satchel of marvels...

But now in an evil time, when every day
brings sirens from the cities and the settlements,
the checkpoints and the roadblocks,
when there's a stranglehold on the Territories
and in my head the parable
of the drowning man
grabbing more than his share of plank,
or the man who jumps from a house on fire
to land on his neighbour's neck, and stays there,
I don't know what to think,

anymore, perhaps, than you;
and when we meet in Paris – the best we can do –
intemperate remarks, overheard
from a neighbouring table,
cast such gloom, I hurry you off
to the Musée Guimet where you found, I think,
some peace among the limestone Buddhas
of the Khmer, with their famous Anghkor Smile,
or at least a pause, before your midnight flight,
as you describe it, back to turmoil.

Now, you translate Halevi in Jerusalem;
amid the chaos stillness, where your pen moves
to retrace a time almost of tolerance
in some Ideal City, the medieval dreamcourts
of Granada, Cordoba, Seville,
where Jew and Arab jousted
in the subtle art of scriptural allusion,
the Hebrew *shibbutz* against the Arab *iqtibas*,
meaning, so your learned Notes inform me,
*The lighting of one flame from another.*

# 5

*An Enthusiast*

*i.m. MLRR (1927–2001)*

*for my sisters*

# Pottering About

A friend, kindly-curious,
asks do I think of you at all
do I miss you

now the winter has left off
and taken you with it
leaving this clearance

this sunny place to be busy in
where everything suddenly is busy
and the light reaches into corners

and into rooms and the space
is taller and more distant,
I want to know why

any sign of neglect or decay
weighs on my conscience
when you were always the one

somewhere at work among the birdsong
and the appleboughs, the place marked
by a stupendous oath

as the Allen Scythe choked
or where the odd chainsaw
was hurled into the undergrowth

and I dreaming on
among my books
in the yellow attic room.

Now my listless gathering
of the vicious acacia branches
strewn across the grass

brings to mind
my reluctant piece-work, the twigs
I brought to your bonfire,

(I didn't really lift a finger)
and here I am, at pause again,
my acreage before me

my crooked trees my crooked cat
my flourishing weeds
my hedges gone haywire:

perhaps if I think hard enough
there you'll be, putting them straight
though not too straight,

and not too perfect,
and with plenty of breaks,
such is the way of us.

# An Enthusiast

Nothing quite dislodged
the early passions, they took possession
hourly, every time my father
walked the marshes, or listened in
to the 'excellent gramophone'
that 'speaks through the wireless'
in his private sitting room,
or weekly without crackle
in the Albert Hall...
*Aetat* sixteen, he decided
school was loathsome
and nothing mattered anyway
but Music, Ornithology,
a boy called Strode, and God.

Fifty years later
some hardnosed specialist
of consciousness and the genome
held forth at table, claiming
to my father's mild protestation
that Bach's St Matthew Passion
is a product of the human brain
like medicine or the washing machine.
'There is no such thing
as divine inspiration'
and I pushing in
to agree, with an eagerness,
with a vanity,
I now detest and regret.

# Corporal Contact

*'Everything about the ree-lay-shun-ship between men and women makes me angry. It's all a fucking balls-up. It might have been organized by the army, or the Ministry of Food.'*

Philip Larkin, July 1943

Austerity days
of 'winning the peace',
Churchill growling on the wireless
and my father doing National Service
a little too late for Action
and excused most activity,
asthma confining him to deskwork
amid mass courts-martial
and futile inspections
by the bloody Brass Hats.

A lonesome weekly escapade
out of camp
to the nearest town included
hand-holdings with strangers,
and the girl in front 'rested her lovely head
in my hands'
a voluptuous hour
of 'corporal contact'
during *Brief Encounter*
in the shadows of the local flea-pit.

## Les Portes de la Nuit

The matinée looks and height
set him apart
in any cinema or theatre foyer
when we sought my father out

on an evening trip to London;
and our family dinner
at Lyons or the Golden Egg
had precedents, I now find,

from his *Strictly Private Diary*
of 1947, when changed from
clammy khaki into coolest civvies
he joined the West End crowds

'feeling pretty lonely'.
He 'had a meal in Lyons'
and went to see a French film,
*Les Portes de la Nuit*,

'where next to me
was a young woman
who was sitting, with her arms bare.
My right hand on which I rested

my left elbow
was touching her right arm.
She left her arm
in that position, and gradually

I increased the pressure of my hand
against her arm and extended
my grasp. Soon she clasped
my hand in hers.

I encircled her shoulders
with my left arm and we sat
clasped together like lovers.
It was very pleasant.'

And when he escorted her outside
he found a good-looking girl
as well-spoken as himself
but nevertheless decided

not to make a firm arrangement
she not striking him
as being the girl, or rather *the* girl
for a closer relationship

though from this time on
there was no desire stronger in his mind
'than to meet and make
the firm friendship

of a girl who might later
become my wife.'
But they kissed on the lips
in any case,

(also pleasant),
and then he left her
and travelled by taxi to Kensington
'mentally dazed'.

A little while conversing
with his grandmother
though his mind elsewhere
and his sleep 'tumultuous'.

'Probably a useful and
steadying experience,
nothing vulgar or immoral,
but my mind disturbed.'

One page later
he's back at Camp,
reading Wundt's *Psychology*
in the Education Hut.


## Brahms


Now I have your diary
it is you as well as I
and we act as one
when Brahms's 2nd Piano Conc.
comes on the radio...
I'm still at school
playing it on my Sanyo
Radio-Cassette Recorder,
or escaping my tormentors
in the darkened Music Room,
skulking round the gramophone
illegally, missing Games,
an outcast of the afternoon
wondering what it might be
to 'fit in', and how it might be done,
when the opening horn announces
there must be something more
than this, this is nothing
and I am no one, except for
the savage, dry euphoria
as the piano surges in.

# Subject to Limitation

For years you were subjected
to a generous selection
of fragments for piano
wafting from the nursery
to your armchair
in the drawing room.

Later you admitted
frustration with your diet
of *Intérruptions musicales*.
Unfailingly the Moonlight
broke down
into a manic doodle.

The promising beginnings!
The assertive chords!
I could sit down now
and play them for you
and then break down
in all the same places.

# Cambridge

Lulled by the sweetness
of my father's protected days:
an extinct species
of male coziness,
boat-club companionship
and muscular Christianity,
days of coldwash and coalfire,
and impassioned tea-parties
listening to Bach,
his *gravitas* on the gramophone.
An earnest of undergraduates
'toasting crumpets and eating cake,
talking 15 to the dozen'.

*Anima naturaliter Christiana*
never doubting the divinity
of Christ 'as fact'
– a certitude that disarms
the chaplain, all limbered up
for strenuous debate
on godhead, and the Church,
on Broad and Low and High –
but the soul remains perplexed
by 'unchristian desires'
solitary in digs, with
Keeton on *Trusts* or
Jenks on *General Principles*.

*Absolute Purity*
is now the mantra,
the young man's Motto,
and God's sure cure
for lust and acne.
A Rule for Living
that doesn't work,
and thus begins
the everlasting tussle

between Freud, the Chaplain
and his own complexion,
with the pained conviction
of impurities in the blood...

One wintry afternoon
my father rises from the couch
of 'amorous conduct'
to hear an 'indifferent sermon'
and then returns
to read around Conflict of Laws
and castigate his taste
for 'debased acquaintance'.
He compiles 'a vast list!',
kneels beside the chaplain
in Little St Mary's,
and feels as expected
the bliss of absolution.

'Tea in the Eros,
talking arrant nonsense
about the colours
of different key signatures!'
And also this:
a Lenten afternoon
in David's, finding a used Anthology,
and determined to master
territory unexplored as yet,
the Art of Poetry, he places it
ceremoniously
in the basket of his bicycle.

(Two weeks later:
'weeping over Wordsworth').

# Frérot

Your glossier brother held court
in well-appointed rooms
where 'Bournvita' would hardly be the thing,
cigars and French liqueur rather,
the younger brother you loved and reproved
for mixing with a dubious set,
*autre* staircase, *autres moeurs*...

Groomed in London, finished in Lausanne,
a photo shows him, posed with cigarette.
He quit the world cruise early, lost
his cash to a cardsharp in Rome,
got a bit 'laced' on his twenty-first,
and met you in Murdoch's, Folkestone,
you to buy Bach, he Mistinguett.

# Christmas Swans at Welney

*'had tea in a converted lifeboat-house...'*

*'I could live there all my life watching birds – though I should want to work after a while.'*

We had the vision,
the vision came on cue, at feeding time,
and much too easy
for your expertise.
It's the epilogue I recall,
our journey from the hide
with son, and grandson
helping you down the hill
suddenly shaky
to the over-heated Visitor Centre
a mean hut with a sickly smell.
A Belling 2-bar! It takes you back
to the NAAFI, where you stood as
Battalion Orderly Corporal
with blanco'd web-belt & gaiters
watching over the swill bin
for 'gross wastage of food'.

It's a long way to come
from one Nissen hut to another
eating thin minestrone
fastidiously like your mother,
shoulders hunched
with that expression
of distaste you put on
for medicine
or the hospital food –
a face unchanged from boyhood.
And the vestigial boyishness
with you even now, whereas
the edgy prig, prone to anger
and quick to judgement
has receded.

A long way to come
from your legal drudgery
in the army
dealing with the desertions
of 1947 (India, *Lolita*, the Marshall Plan),
waking the conventional
man of law within you
and intent on your own discoveries
*broadening your horizons*
– preferring to dances
the Education Hut,
'I tried to listen to the Emperor Concerto
but was driven out
by the childish noisiness
of the librarians'...

Or a weekend on the mudflats
of Norfolk, taking tea
in a converted lifeboat
with your life before you,
its idea of heaven now indelible,
the open marshes
'dunlin, plover, knot, godwits & sanderling'
your heart in hiding
'away with the birds', in the arch
diction of your diary, where you
'partake of meals'
and 'amiable converse'
but are happiest striding out
on thundering Dungeness
an awkward young man
intense and lonely
worried by your height
abundantly pimpled
beneath the itching Khaki
and longing, now,
for a *proper fiancée*, release,
and the demob suit,
but listless still, and fearful
of stepping out
in Civvy Street.

## Straws

Too weak now to suck on a straw
my father clutches at straws:
'Leave no stone unturned.'

When I consulted with his doctors
behind a curtain
he saw our gathered shadows

and Sister said in forthright terms
you should go home,
there's nothing we can do for you...

At the close of my visit
and the amiable converse
as he would put it

I kiss him briefly on the forehead
– as he would do, and leave my door ajar,
and go downstairs for supper.

# Drawing the Fire

Kneeling on the stained concrete floor
shoveling out the tiered ash
to feed the new stove,
crushing paper in its maw
I thought how you would draw the fire
stooping from your considerable height
to the small hearth
where you spread a page
of the broadsheet *Times*
that bellied inward
with a whoosh and roar.

I watched astonished at how long
the furnace orange
glowed without catching
or breaking through
– until it did, and with an oath
you stuffed the whole thing
sparking up the chimney flue;
and then I'd lie full length
through my teens and twenties
head against the footstool
roasting gently on one side

through years of soaps and news.
Home from work, peering in,
you'd laugh and say unfailingly
*The great feast goes on*, but never
*Have you nothing else to do?*
my idleness somehow reassuring…
And in summer, the curtains drawn
for Wimbledon,
there was the sweet smell of soot
and flowers in the particled light
of that yellow room.

Now in my *hameau abattu*
where the wine flows
out of hard graft and frozen flint
the angelus has fallen silent.
I stoop to feed the fire
and think of you
and your considerable height
providing what I never thought of,
more than enough
of light and water
food and drink.

# Fixing the Angle

He fixes the angle
            of the daybed
and now my father's feet
            are higher than his head
pointing up the chancel
            to the East
beyond the silhouette of trees
            I watch my eyes
sink in their sockets
            like his, like his

Fixing the angle
            on the daybed
I see him
            I become him
a gesture repeated
            brings him home
(never again)
            to watch the water
a dance of
            oblongs oblongs oblongs
entranced by the word
            and why not
for the hours
            spent supine
as the oblongs trembled
            and why not
as near a state
            to blessedness
as any, as near
            a world of light

He squints
            to make me out
where I stand
            remote at his bedside
his 20/20 vision
            fading as I look
at his unlikeness

# Be Prepared

My father's feet
are higher than his head
on his hydraulic hi-tech bed.
He floats in and out
of surrounding 'conversazione'
on a crest of Bach
or in a pool of Albinoni,
slipping in and out of the *News*
in and out
of the ordinary day
anything and everything
from *You & Yours*
to the *Archers*,
nothing admitted
or given away.

And then an absence –
the morning *Times* crisp, unopened,
but nothing much yet to report,
another catastrophic Test,
a hold-up in the Talks...
His motto was *Be Prepared*...
Strange then that nonchalance
at the end, a revenge
on all things legal,
on his horse-haired genitors on the stairs,
and the family language of
*clauses providing for,*
for when the time came
the Clauses were unconcluded,
the Instructions unclear.

## No Interruptions

I cannot wholly decide
about my father's resolve not to speak

or seek out texts
or make arrangements

except perhaps to the pillow
and the blankets.

Was it for him, or for us,
or was he 'in denial'

when he preferred to drift and doze
to music or ambient conversation

as if some unusual act
would make the thing too real?

That adherence to routine,
*The Times* and the radio, was it

because the stream of time
remained too precious to interrupt early,

as when he waited for the concert to end
before unfolding himself from the car?

## 'Lord I believe! Help Thou my unbelief.'

Is it because lifelong
your belief was firm
you spoke about it little,

was it a hard conviction
or a hardened conviction
that lay unquestioned,

and my impertinence
is in asking this now
when anyway you cannot answer.

Was yours the personal god
searching you out as you sought him
and once found, found forever?

A young man, raw and gangly,
the faith was your own and proof
against your sceptical father

who taunted you with an oath
*Christ's Trousers!* and an impish urge
to ruffle a son grown pious.

And then the group of prayerful friends
many of whom moved on, to therapy
or progressive thinking, but never you

with your unsounded
indubitable refuge
that proved almost a mystery.

Opaque, untouchable; a thing
like Father Christmas, we could never
openly admit to disbelieving

for fear of disappointing you,
and so the same thing later on
learning not to press too hard.

But latterly
in this rebellion of your body
did belief founder

or were you incredulous
perhaps until the very end
propped in the hospice bed

where you intoned the Eucharist loud and clear
and sat up rigid and laid down the law
the ancestors in you

speaking for the very last time
which was rare, for someone
who so hated 'sticking out';

or would you agree, a lifetime
of belief, and of guarding
silently your unbelief?

## Magistrate

At the end he sat bolt upright
and read the riot act
to an empty ward:

hooligans and vandals
came back to haunt
his closing statement.

# Further Encounters

The closest we ever were
was a silence facing each other
across the drawing room
in the strict arc of the chairs

*Mache dich mein Herze rein*
*Ich will Jesum selbst begraben*

Bach the evangelist ebbed and flowed

and at my back
a crowd of thorns at the window

The two of us rigid unable to speak
or move again least of all
look each other in the eye
I can't remember
who blinked first or why

★ ★ ★ ★

Something of the grey heron
the ashen heron
in your demeanour
when you stood watching herons

– nowhere more so than in that photo
one of the last
where wasting visibly
on that extreme Australian reserve

you took yourself off to
in a further removal
you are standing tall
amongst your leggy waders

★ ★ ★ ★

Leaving the moated lady
who lives where the rivers rise
and where the heron fishes
on the sandbank at the cross-current

I met you on the track in your medium
and nothing could grow old anymore
while the balsam cotton was falling
slowly towards and past me forever

## Striking Out

...As if one dusk he veered
into thickets
to find, once and for all,
the place of the oriole.

He was always swerving
dangerously, to get a look
at a roadside hawk, or darting
into woods, only this time

he went further in...
Something a little unusual,
like last night, when I struck out
to poach a few bluebells

and found the wood barred.
Some forthright soul
had hung a banner at the entrance
announcing TRAPS

– and I went in
holding a sapper's stick
half in mockery, half in fear
of the torch and the dog

(but this must be unlike
the drifting out –
this was adrenaline, stealth,
staying alive).

# Not HIP

Not in the end our style, we must admit,
the 'historically informed performance'
wheezing and scraping and treadling away...

Rather the clobbering big sound,
Klemperer's *Largo Largo Largo*
and the massed choirs rising.

# Markie

*'...but the grandest sight of the day was seeing the battalion advance, the men dancing along, only too anxious to get to close grips with the enemy. All behaved gallantly...'*
Kings Royal Rifle Corps Chronicle, 7th Battalion War Records, 1916

Markie's pencil in the glass table,
with medals, cups, memorial coins,
knick-knacks of the drawing room

open to our hushed curiosity
along with figs grown in hankies
and the Coca-Cola soda-maker...

MLRR, your initials, and your lost uncle's,
'mortally wounded' in 1916
between Longueval and Flers.

Scarcely spoken of, he wasn't shot
in front of your father's eyes
as family dramatics has it:

brothers were kept in separate trenches.
His details were waiting
on the War Graves website,

Name/Rank/Regt/Battalion/ –
and we are the 'third generation',
grandsons to process memories...

'There's a lot of interest now'
goes the chirpy voice on the telephone
in answer to my inquiry.

'He mightn't have died in a major assault,
it could have been sniper, accident,
anything…' 'That's OK' I replied.

His parents received the Field Postcard,
the 'wounded' line applies.
His mother's day-book stops.

# Littlestone Days

After the golf, the bridge & the cocktails,
after the sets of tennis
with Noel Coward & the Maughams
looking on from a balcony,
'ah, the dear boys!',
after sherry and theatricals,
the dinner-dances and the outings,
after charades and canasta
and evenings with the gramophone,

you alone of them would turn your back
and cycle into the wind, then stride
your giant stride across that sacred name,
Dungeness, hiss of a withdrawing sea
across the shingle, the bitter waters,
exulting, sacred music perpetually
on your tongue
as you trudged to the Point
sobbing your pent-up grief-and-happiness

into the wind, for God's abundant mercies,
in giving you such friends,
and this wilderness to walk alone in.
That is how I would greet you – had I
the courage, had I anything like the presence –
on your returning from an afternoon,
a bird count, having yet again
renounced temptation
out there on the marshes!

## Threading it all...

Threading it all, and shadowing
the triumphs
is something more deeply unsure:

the intermittent crises
of self-esteem, the struggle,
at times despairing, against failure

and self-exclusion, the need
that another's vitality
enliven him,

the sorrowful walks
of a soul uncynical
in the extreme.

# Rare Visitor

The Peggotty house, upturned wreck,
a caravan-cum-igloo, nursery railway,
a bucket of shingle and drift,
immutable fishermen,
tarred soles, upright sleepers,
the lavateria the common ragwort
where cinnabar caterpillars feed
turning strangely from black and yellow
to black and red and winged;
where he scoured
the ballast pit and the willows for migrants
she hurries through the gorse
through ragwort
and viper's bugloss
the teasels the broom
the purple loosestrife
I name them in trust
the tormentil sweet alison
looking for the lakes
that have wandered, apparently;
and on this anniversary
they haven't heard of him
round here
he has left it all to us,
the nuclear light, the unlikely heat,
the fissures in the carapace,
the brand-new, child-friendly, hands-on Observatory
a short walk from the car-park.

## After Fifty-Four Years

The darling girl
in velvet and satin
who fitted in
so well,

the sweet girl
you kissed
on the doorstep
after the show,

read your secret
loving words
tonight.
That's all I know.

# Selected titles from the Oxford*Poets* list

Oxford*Poets*, an imprint of Carcanet Press, celebrates the vitality and diversity of contemporary poetry in English.

**Joseph Brodsky** *Collected Poems in English*
For Brodsky, to be a poet was an absolute, a total necessity...scintillating deployment of language, and always tangential or odd ways of interpreting ideas, events or other literature. John Kinsella, OBSERVER

**Greg Delanty** *Collected Poems 1986–2006*
A body of work that has grown steadily from book to book in depth, invention, and ambition. AGENDA

**Jane Draycott** *The Night Tree*
Hers is a scrupulous intelligence...Her searching curiosity and wonderful assurance make her an impeccable and central poetic intelligence. Penelope Shuttle, MANHATTAN REVIEW

**Sasha Dugdale** *The Estate*
Dugdale creates a spare, mythical tone that fits itself perfectly to the elemental Russian landscape in which much of her collection is set. GUARDIAN

**Rebecca Elson** *A Responsibility to Awe*
This is a wise and haunting volume, which I can't recommend too warmly. Boyd Tonkin, INDEPENDENT

**Marilyn Hacker** *Essays on Departure*
Everything is thrilling and true, fast and witty, deep and wise; her vitality is the pulse of life itself. Derek Mahon

**Peter Scupham** *Collected Poems*
The sophistication of the technique which underpins every poem becomes clearer and clearer as you read further in this substantial, generous, distinguished volume. Peter Davidson, Books of the Year 2005, READYSTEADYBOOK.COM

**Charles Tomlinson** *Cracks in the Universe*
Tomlinson is a unique voice in contemporary English poetry, and has been a satellite of excellence for the past 50 years. David Morley, GUARDIAN

**Marina Tsvetaeva** *Selected Poems*, trans. **Elaine Feinstein**
Feinstein has performed the first, indispensable task of a great translator: she has captured a voice. THREEPENNY REVIEW

**Chris Wallace-Crabbe** *By and Large*
His allies are words, and he sues them with the care of a surgeon and the flair of a conjuror. Peter Porter

Visit **www.carcanet.co.uk** to browse a complete list of Oxford*Poets* and Carcanet titles, find out about forthcoming books and order books at discounted prices.

Email **info@carcanet.co.uk** to subscribe to the Carcanet e-letter for poetry news, events and a poem of the week.